OTHER BOOKS BY THIS AUTHOR:

Seder to Sunday
Step into Scripture
A Bible Study for Easter

The Book on Bullies: Break Free in Forty
(40 Minutes or 40 Days)
Includes 40 Devotionals to Fortify Your Soul

The Book on Bullies
How to Handle Them Without Becoming One of Them

THE CHRISTMAS STORY STEP INTO SCRIPTURE

A BIBLE STUDY FOR ADVENT

SUSAN K. BOYD

WESTBOW
PRESS®
A DIVISION OF THOMAS NELSON
& ZONDERVAN

WestBow Press books may be ordered through booksellers or by contacting:

WestBow Press
A Division of Thomas Nelson & Zondervan
1663 Liberty Drive
Bloomington, IN 47403
www.westbowpress.com
1 (866) 928-1240

Because of the dynamic nature of the Internet, any web addresses or links contained in this book may have changed since publication and may no longer be valid. The views expressed in this work are solely those of the author and do not necessarily reflect the views of the publisher, and the publisher hereby disclaims any responsibility for them.

Any people depicted in stock imagery provided by Getty Images are models, and such images are being used for illustrative purposes only. Certain stock imagery © Getty Images.

All Scripture quotations, unless otherwise indicated, are taken from the Holy Bible, New International Version®, NIV®. Copyright ©1973, 1978, 1984, 2011 by Biblica, Inc.™ Used by permission of Zondervan. All rights reserved worldwide. www.zondervan.com The "NIV" and "New International Version" are trademarks registered in the United States Patent and Trademark Office by Biblica, Inc.™

Scripture marked (KJV) taken from the King James Version of the Bible.

ISBN: 978-1-9736-7692-8 (sc)
ISBN: 978-1-9736-7691-1 (hc)
ISBN: 978-1-9736-7693-5 (e)

Library of Congress Control Number: 2019915762

Print information available on the last page.

WestBow Press rev. date: 11/22/2019

To my granddaughter and grandson—I love you! I enjoy watching you accomplish the amazing things you do. Dedicated to the Lord, committed to excellence, and you're a whole lot of fun. I believe God has big plans for you both.

God so loved the world that he gave his one and only Son that whoever believes in him shall not perish but have eternal life (John 3:16).

CONTENTS

PREFACE

I wrote *Seder to Sunday—Step into Scripture, A Bible Study for Easter* in 2018. It was the first in the *Step into Scripture Bible Study Series*. I'm very grateful for the feedback shared by individuals and churches that used this study. I am excited people are putting themselves into scenes of Biblical history and applying that experience to their circumstances today. Below you will understand what I hope for the readers of this new study.

The Christmas Story—Step into Scripture is the second Bible Study in this interactive series. Every December, live nativity scenes and pageants draw crowds who stand out in the cold to experience what it might have been like witnessing the advent of Christ. *The Christmas Story—Step into Scripture* is your opportunity to get close to the action with your imagination, intellect and heart.

For instance, step through a hole in time. Experience up close and personal all Mary and Joseph may be thinking and feeling at this pivotal point in their lives. How does young Mary feel being informed by an angel that she will be the mother of the Son of God? What is going through Joseph's mind hearing his beloved Mary is pregnant but not with his child? Will he believe an angel who says this baby is God's son? Step out of Scripture and come back to today for this question: Can you remember a time when you had to trust God even when common sense told you otherwise?

When groups are identified in the Bible you have the opportunity to join them! This gives you a closer look and deeper insight. For example, *you are* one of the shepherds watching over your sheep in the hills of Bethlehem. Shepherds lead a somewhat isolated life outdoors. You are marginalized in your community. You are not allowed to be a witness in court as society believes you to be less than credible. So why are you down in the town, telling people in the streets about a night sky filled with angels and the baby king you found in a manger? How important do you feel tonight, being given the *only personal invitation* from the God of the Universe to celebrate and see his newborn son?

You are now part of *The Christmas Story—Step into Scripture, A Bible Study for Advent!*

INTRODUCTION

Would you do a Bible study if it were as exciting as watching a play or movie? *The Christmas Story—Step into Scripture, A Bible Study for Advent* is your invitation to time travel and walk through the pages of biblical history. As you decide what you think, do, and feel as a shepherd, citizen of Jerusalem, or the powerful and admired magi, the Bible will come to life in front of you.

Here are some tips on how to gain the most from this interactive Bible study.

Imagine you can watch and listen to Joseph and Mary. Closer than simply reading about them, you use Scripture to evaluate their reactions to events.

Spend time studying the background of some of these people. Who were the mysterious magi? Why were they considered wise men? Was Herod the Great actually great? Refer to the *Note* section to get all the historical information.

Take a moment to read a *Scene* section that paints the setting so you can place yourself there. Except for the *Note* section, the study is written in the present tense. The question will not be "What did they do then?" Instead it will read, "What are you doing, now?"

If you are enjoying this Bible study with a group, don't skip any of it. *Read the Scene, Note, and questions aloud together.* Remember in order to imagine you are stepping through a hole in time, you will all need to see the same scene and everything behind the scene. That helps you decide what you think, feel, or do in that verse while you are living in that place and time.

Be encouraged if you think you are without imagination. You don't need much! The Bible study is the director here to assist you. Thoughts or feelings of a character may occasionally be suggested by the author. It helps the reader understand motives and actions. This adds texture and color to the characters. Nothing, however, is added unless Scripture or authoritative commentaries give facts that would substantiate details appearing in the picture.

Do the question that reads, "Step out of Scripture, and come back to today." This is usually a two-or three-part question at the end of each lesson, and it will help you make applications to your life.

Notice pictures and poems which are always featured in the Step into Scripture Bible Study Series. Pictures are included so you can better visualize verses. Poems are meant to inspire personal reflection reinforcing and following each lesson.

I hope enjoying *The Christmas Story—Step into Scripture* makes the advent of Christ and all the events surrounding his coming the most exciting part of your Christmas this year!

In the beginning was the word, and the Word was with God, and the Word was God. He was with God in the beginning. Through him all things were made; without him nothing was made that has been made. In him was life, and that life was the light of mankind. The light shines in the darkness and the darkness has not overcome it (John 1:1-5).

MARY: MESSIAH'S MOTHER-TO-BE

LUKE 1

Note

Israel is not the promised land Abraham imagined. It is no longer the land of milk and honey. King Solomon's days of splendor are long past. Israel is occupied by Rome. The year is between 4 and 6 BC.[1] Roman soldiers march through the streets. No Elijah rallies the people, and no Moses is in sight to lead them out of captivity. *And for four hundred years, God has been silent.*

Scene

Jewish parents tuck children into bed next to them and tell stories of David and Goliath. They reassure their little ones, "Someday God will raise up the Messiah from the line of David to save his people, Israel!" Every child and adult in the nation dreams for that day. Mary and Joseph have heard the stories and hold the same hope to someday see the Messiah (Isaiah 11:1–5). (Note that Jesse, named in Isaiah 11:1, was the father of King David.)

Mary, a teenager, recently was betrothed (married) to Joseph. Joseph is older than Mary and already working as a carpenter. Joseph's family pay her parents the customary *mohar*, which is like a reverse dowry.[2] This money could help with the cost of the wedding.

The couple is considered married. However, they will be expected to live celibate lives separately in their own family homes for one year before the actual wedding. Mary knows this is society's testing of both their faithfulness to one another and their patience, as they wait this full year before coming together.

Meanwhile, Joseph will build their home. Mary can prepare for her wedding day. Friends and neighbors will begin looking forward to celebrating with the couple.

Note

Today, God is no longer silent in Israel!

1. Explain the conversation between Zechariah and the angel of God (Luke 1:5–22).

2. How does Elizabeth give glory to God (Luke 1:23–25)?

3. How far along in her pregnancy is Elizabeth when the angel visits Mary (Luke 1:26)?

4. What message does Gabriel the angel give to Mary (Luke 1:26–33)? Match a prophecy to each promise given by the angel of God (Isaiah 7:14; 9:6–7; Psalm 2:2–7; 45:6–7; 89:26–29; 2 Samuel 7:16).

5. Describe Mary's initial reaction (Luke 1:29–34).

6. How does Gabriel encourage Mary (Luke 1:35–37)?

7. Read Isaiah 7:14, which details the prophecy given centuries before Mary was born. How does this prove Gabriel's statement "For no word from God will ever fail" (Luke 1:37)?

8. Trace Mary's move from fear to faith. What impresses you most about her final statement to Gabriel and ultimately to God (Luke 1:38)?

9. **Step out of Scripture, and come back to today for this question. (This is a three-part question.)**

What surprising turn of events are you facing today?

List questions you have for the Lord about your future?

Write down verses that serve as an encouragement to you. Look through the Psalms for promises that God is with you in your circumstance.

FROM FEAR TO FAITH: MARY

When confusion is untangled
There is peace. I understand,
All questions no longer matter,
If I can be in God's plan.

Everything impossible
Becomes a reality,
And the future not yet lived,
I can face with certainty.

At this moment God's presence
Fills this empty space.
No room left for misgivings,
Love just took its place.

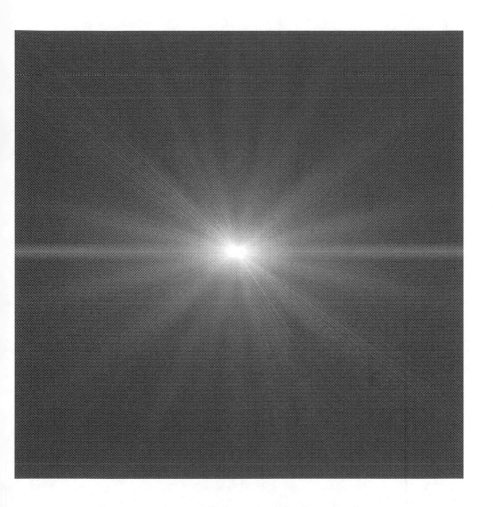

The people walking in darkness have seen a great light; on those living in the land of the shadow of death a light has dawned (Isaiah 9:2).

LESSON 2

MARY & ELIZABETH CELEBRATE TOGETHER

LUKE 1:39–56

Note

Travel sounds instantaneous in the Bible. In one verse someone departs, and in the next verse, that person arrives. This is the case when Mary "got ready and hurried to a town in the hill country in Judea" to see her relative Elizabeth (Luke 1:39–40). But the fact is she may have had the early symptoms of morning sickness, and the "hill country" mentioned in scripture was the Judean mountains. Though probably in a caravan, her trip from Nazareth to Judea didn't end for a hundred miles![1] Nevertheless, nothing seemed to dampen Mary's excitement to share with Elizabeth. Afterall, the angel Gabriel is the one who inspired her to find out more about Elizabeth's miraculous pregnancy!

1. Do you think Mary spends time during her journey thinking about how she will explain her pregnancy to Elizabeth? What do you imagine is going through her mind?

2. What is Elizabeth's greeting to her younger cousin? Where do you think Elizabeth gets her insight about the origin of Mary's baby (Luke 1:17; 1:39–44)?

3. How is Elizabeth quickly becoming Mary's mentor and encourager (Luke 1:42–45)?

Note

Mary responds by reciting a song and praising God for favoring her and her people (Luke 1:46–55). It is known as "The Magnificat," and it is filled with Old

Testament allusions and quotations. It is similar to Zechariah's prayer in Luke 1:67–79 and Hanna's song in 1 Samuel 2:1–10.[2]

4. **Step out of Scripture, and come back to today for this question.** Make a list of all God's attributes or deeds for which Mary praises the Lord. Try praising God by reading aloud parts of the Magnificat before giving him your list of prayer requests each day this week. Evaluate at the end of the week if praising God has helped you appreciate him more.

5. How far along is Mary's pregnancy when she finally goes home (Luke 1:56)?

6. List all the problems Mary knows she will face upon her return home. How has she been strengthened and helped by spending time with someone who understands her situation?

7. **Step out of Scripture, and come back to today for this question. (This is a three-part question.)**

What words from a friend have inspired you the most?

When have you, like Mary, felt understood and supported by a friend without having to explain your situation?

How could you and a friend encourage each other in the Lord?

Note

Though John and Jesus were relatives, as boys they never met (John 1:31)! Did their mothers tell them the miraculous stories of their conceptions or God's mission for their lives? Scripture is silent on these points.

Before leaving this lesson, step through a hole in time, and go into the future thirty years to the banks of the Jordan River in Israel.

Crowds from everywhere wade into the water to be baptized by the man known as John the Baptist. He had been the baby inside Elizabeth, who leaped for joy when Mary first approached her cousin, carrying the Messiah within her. Now John, these many years later, is as honored when Jesus comes to be baptized by him as his mother was to be visited by Mary. Elizabeth, long ago, had greeted Mary in a loud voice as she exclaimed, "Blessed are you among women and blessed is the child you will bear! But why am I so favored that the mother of my Lord should come to me?" (Luke 1:42–43).

Now, John, like his mother had done so many years ago, describes how privileged he feels in the presence of the Son of God:

A person can receive only what is given them from heaven. You yourselves can testify that I said, 'I am not the Messiah but am sent ahead of him.' The Bride belongs to the bridegroom. The friend who attends the bridegroom waits and listens for him, and is full of joy when he hears the bridegroom's voice. That joy is mine and is now complete. He must become greater: I must become less (John 3:27–30).

When John sees Jesus coming toward him, he exclaims, "Look the Lamb of God, who takes away the sin of the world" (John 1:29).

FRIENDSHIP

"Iron sharpens iron,"
I know the Scriptures say,
"There's a friend that's closer than a brother,"
I need to be that today.

Instead of feeling I'm alone,
With responsibility,
Am I the encourager,
Keeping you company?

Can you count on me
To listen from the heart,
And be your confidant,
And take your part?

Mary came to Elizabeth.
Jesus could trust John.
Together, my friend, we'll lean on the Lord.
He's compassionate and strong.

The true light that gives light to everyone
was coming into the world (John 1:9)

JOSEPH TAKES MARY AS WIFE

MATTHEW 1:18-25

Scene

Mary is more than three months pregnant when she arrives back in her hometown, Nazareth. Joseph discovers she is with child. He is sick at heart. He may be thinking, *I waited for her. I was faithful. Why wasn't she? Where has she been, and who was she with?* He can't bring himself to ask her any of these questions.

Joseph struggles within himself. If he takes Mary as his wife into his home, then people will either think that he was intimate with her before she left Nazareth or that he is a fool to raise another man's child. Either way, he loses face with people he has known all his life.

Then as his hurt turns to anger, he stops and realizes that whatever her reasons for doing what she did, she is in harm's way now. He knows if he accuses her of infidelity, then by law she can be stoned. He has no good choices, and none of this is his fault. But Joseph cares for Mary and feels protective of her. He wants to help her, so he pushes aside his hurt. He considers giving her a writ of divorce quietly. Then no one would have the right to stone her. That means he is not admitting or denying that the child is his. Again, he can see no good choices.

1. How would you describe Joseph's character (Matthew 1:18–19)? List some of Joseph's attributes that you imagine God would want in the man who will be raising his Son.

2. What do you think Joseph is feeling? What has he decided to do about Mary (Matthew 1:19)?

3. Who changes his mind (Matthew 1:20–21; Isaiah 7:14)? How?

4. With what title is Joseph addressed by the angel in his dream, serving as evidence that he is definitely in the kingly, messianic line (though he will not be related by blood to Jesus) (Matthew 1:20)?

5. Explain the significance of the names of the Son of God (Jeremiah 23:5–6; Matthew 1:20–23). Which details about the child's origin comfort Joseph (Matthew 1:20–23; Isaiah 7:14)? (Note that the meaning of Jesus's *names* are as follows: Jesus means Savior or Jehovah's salvation. Immanuel, which is also spelled Emmanuel, means "God with us." Messiah means God's anointed one, and Christ is Greek for Messiah.)

6. Describe how Joseph went from indecision to action at God's Word (Matthew 1:19–24).

7. In what ways does Joseph immediately demonstrate his respect for God and his care for Mary and her child (Matthew 1:24–25)?

8. **Step out of Scripture, and come back to today for this question. (This is a two-part question.)**

Can you remember a time when you had to trust God when common sense told you otherwise?

How is God helping you care more about what *He wants* than what other people think?

INTEGRITY:

Joseph,
Stepfather of the Christ

Character under stress,
Injury without complaint,
Selfless consideration,
Love without constraint.

"I have come into the world as a light so that no one who believes in me should stay in darkness" (John 12:46).

JESUS, THE SAVIOR, IS BORN

LUKE 2:1–7

Note

Caesar Augustus commanded a census be taken over the entire Roman Empire. This was done to keep track of the population and help with taxation. However, in God's plan Mary and Joseph were going to the very place that prophecy predicted the Messiah would be born—the city of Bethlehem. "But you, Bethlehem Ephrathah, though you are small among the clans of Judah, out of you will come for me, one who will be ruler over Israel, whose origins are from old, from ancient days" (Micah 5:2).

Ancestry and genealogy were extremely important, perhaps more to the Jews of the day than even to the Roman government. Jews kept track of their lineage until AD 70, when all public records were destroyed along with Jerusalem. For instance, before AD 70, a Levite priest had to prove his unbroken lineage back to Aaron.

If a man had the slightest mixture of foreign blood, he lost his right to be called a Jew. Even the Jewish historian Josephus listed his pedigree first, which he said he found in the public record, before writing his autobiography.[1]

Any claim to be the Messiah meant public records could trace that person's genealogy back to King David. Records were available to support Mary's biological Davidic lineage (Luke 3:21–37). Though Joseph was not the biological father of Jesus, he was the legal father and a direct descendant of King David with the records to prove it (Matthew 1:1–17).[2]

1. Why are Joseph and Mary required by the census to go to Bethlehem particularly (Luke 2:4)?

2. The trip from Nazareth to Bethlehem takes ten days and ninety grueling miles of traveling over rough terrain.[3] Because of her late-stage pregnancy, Mary rides a donkey.[4] What do you imagine the hardships are for Joseph and his nine-month-pregnant wife? Name some of the hazards they are facing along the way.

Scene

The streets of Bethlehem are noisy and crowded with people reporting there for the census. Because no guesthouses are available, Mary and Joseph search until they find a cave (a barn carved out of the side of a hill) behind an inn just in time for the baby to arrive![5] Family is far away. No midwife will be helping them. Friends will not be here to rejoice with them, and no supportive neighbors to lend a hand. They are alone, probably on the outskirts of town. Only livestock, including their own donkey, keep them company.

3. What do you think is going through their minds as they deliver the baby themselves (Luke 2:1–7)?

4. How does their loneliness or difficulties turn into joy as they look into the little face of God's miracle?

5. As Mary finishes nursing her baby, what do you imagine she and Joseph are thinking and feeling?

Scene

Joseph cleans out a manger in the stable. He fills it with the cleanest straw he can find to make a bed for the tiny infant. He pats the little mattress together, pulling out loose straw pieces that could poke the child. The couple brought soft cloths with them, and they tear these into strips to swaddle (wrap around) the baby they have cleaned and fed. Joseph covers the new-found straw with his cloak, which hangs over the sides of the manger.

The gentle man lowers baby Jesus slowly out of his strong carpenter's arms into the makeshift cradle. He drapes his outer robe over Mary to keep her warm. Joseph is attentive to all the needs of his little family, keeping vigil most of the night. Mary watches her husband, appreciating him more every moment.

Note

Swaddling is a wrapping process using strips of cloth around the baby (Luke 2:12 NKJV). This keeps the infant snug and cozy. Swaddling newborns was a common practice. This was done not only to make them feel warm and secure as the wrapping was fairly tight, but it was thought to help promote health and strength and straighten limbs.[6]

6. Describe the high and low points of the last twenty-four hours for this family.

7. **Step out of Scripture, and come back to today for this question. (This is a three-part question.)**

When did the Lord give you strength to go that extra mile?

How is God showing you his provision when you have few resources left?

Who is Jesus (John 1:1–5, 9–14)?

NATIVITY AND ME

Before Mary or Joseph, you existed,
Cocreator with the Father above.
Your light penetrated the darkness,
Your plan inspired by love.

You came to us as a baby,
Then later on to the cross,
You took sin from the sinner,
Giving hope to the lost.

Like Mary and Joseph, I have questions.
Lord, you answer them patiently,
So I must now ask myself this question,
"Who are you to me?"

Yet I am writing you a new command; its truth is seen in him and you, because the darkness is passing, and the true light is already shining (I John 2:8).

SHEPHERDS: GUESTS BY DIVINE INVITATION

LUKE 2:8-20

Scene

The sun is setting behind the hills overlooking Bethlehem. You and the other shepherds draw the sheep in closer to protect them from predators. Each shepherd walks through his flock, sliding his rod across each animal's back to examine carefully for injuries. You are all living with your sheep and have been moving them around the hillsides to graze.

During the rainy season, you find a cave where the sheep can sleep at night and you can rest at the opening, which shepherds call "the gate." You become the *gatekeeper* so that none of your curious lambs will get out, and no hungry animal can get past you. However, when the weather is nice and the grass is green and nourishing, you will live outdoors with your sheep. You sleep lighter, but take turns with your friends, the other shepherds, to watch over the flocks at night.

Like you, these men own and know every lamb and sheep. The sheep know their own shepherd and will follow him even if other flocks of sheep are close by. Your sheep know your voice and become calm at night once they hear you sing or talk to them.

You have seen shepherds who were hired to herd flocks, but they are sometimes careless with the sheep. At the first sign of danger, they leave and come back only when the wild animals are gone. But by then the weakest lambs have become victims. You have watched and known both types of shepherds through your years in these fields.

You like the sense of history you feel whenever you are tending sheep here. These were David's pastures on the outskirts of his hometown. The shepherd who became the greatest king of Israel, was from Bethlehem. Called "a man after God's own heart" (1 Samuel 13:14), David has been the subject of many campfire discussions among you and your friends.

You play the same instruments David played to quiet the flocks at night. Like David, you fight off predators with your rod, sling and stones, and pull back endangered lambs with your staff. You run to upright a sheep if it rolls over too far on its back, which all the shepherds know as being *cast* or *downcast*. Sheep are not able to right themselves and can die if a shepherd does not notice and put them quickly back on their feet.[1] You recognize and enjoy the rich shepherd language in David's psalm, as you recall his words, "Why are you downcast O my soul put your hope in God, for I will yet praise him, my Savior and my God" (Psalm 42:5).

You believe David would have understood you. He cared for his sheep and his people. Did being a shepherd make him a better leader? It might have been a good training ground, but you wonder if he had to suffer the humiliations that you and your friends endure now.

Shepherds are considered disreputable and unclean by today's social standards.[2] You lack credibility simply because your occupation is shepherding. Men in your line of work are not allowed to testify in court. People believe all your time alone creates an unreliable storyteller.

Shepherds are out of sight and out of mind, which is how most people prefer it. As you think about all of this, you remember a story of David being out of sight and out of mind too.

When David was a shepherd boy, his family forgot him! One day the prophet Samuel came to their house to anoint one of Jesse's sons as the next king of Israel. After seven sons filed past Samuel, the prophet exclaimed, "The Lord has not chosen these. Are these all your sons?" Finally, David's father said, "There is still the youngest. He is tending the sheep" (I Samuel 16:9-12).

And Samuel anointed David, the shepherd boy, as king.

You look up at the stars. You wonder if you are forgotten and where you fit into God's plan. Then you smile as you look down on the town of Bethlehem. You know the Messiah is predicted to come as a descendant of David, the shepherd king. After all, Bethlehem was the town of David. You say to yourself, "God decides who is important, not man."

1. What are you abruptly seeing in front of you and all around you in the hills of Bethlehem (Luke 2:8–9)? Describe your first thought and response to all you see?

2. Find five encouraging proclamations the angel gives you (Luke 2:10–11). Give the one that takes away your terror and the statement that moves you to action?

3. List the three names given to Jesus by the angel and what they mean to you (Luke 2:11). Describe the sign the angel gives you (Luke 2:12). (Note that shepherds frequently swaddled baby lambs to keep their fleece clean before taking them to the temple.)

4. How many angels arrive, and what is their praise to God and encouragement to you (Luke 2:13-14)?

5. What is your reaction and that of your friends after the angels leave (Luke 2:15)? Describe your conversation.

6. Are you running through the streets, knocking on doors, or did you come upon the open stable and spot the baby wrapped up in a manger (Luke 2:16)?

7. Describe the details you are telling everyone and their responses (Luke 2:17–18).

8. How important do you feel tonight, being given the *only personal invitation* from the God of the universe to celebrate and see his newborn Son (Luke 2:17–20)?

9. **Step out of Scripture, and come back to today for this question. (This is a three-part question.)**

Have you ever felt invisible?

Are you like the shepherds and excited about what you are discovering? If so, with whom do you want to share this?

You might be surprised as the shepherds possibly were, to discover you were never invisible to God. Are you reluctant or willing to follow the Good Shepherd when he calls you?

Note

The Old and New Testaments alike contain many verses that speak of God as the Shepherd and his people as his sheep. But nowhere in Scripture is there a more moving picture of that relationship than in John 10.

Step through a hole in time, and go into the future thirty years. Listen as Jesus, the long-awaited Messiah, offers himself as the true shepherd to his sheep. Here are some excerpts from that chapter:

The one who enters by the gate is the shepherd of the sheep. The gatekeeper opens the gate for him, and the sheep listen to his voice. He calls his own sheep by name and leads them out. When he has brought out all his own sheep, he goes on ahead of them, and his sheep follow him because they know his voice. (John 10:2–4)

I am the good shepherd. The good shepherd lays down his life for the sheep. The hired hand is not the shepherd and does not own the sheep. So, when he sees the wolf coming, he abandons the sheep and runs away. (John 10:11–12)

I am the good shepherd; I know my sheep and my sheep know me. Just as the Father knows me and I know the Father—and I lay down my life for the sheep. (John 10:14–15)

A LAMB'S LOOK AT THE SHEPHERD
(JOHN 10)

I was in the sheepfold.
The shepherd called outside the door,
"I am going to take you some place."
He called my name. Then called once more.

Reluctantly, I stepped outside,
And he pointed with his staff
To a hill so far away from here,
Out of fear I almost laughed!

"I will not go out there alone."
Though I want to be his lamb,
I shook my head and stood my ground.
Then he touched me with his hand.

He stepped out from behind me
And began to lead the way
And commanded, "Stay close to my footsteps,
With your eyes on me today."

Before I realized, we were there,
And the hill was a luscious green
With a view of all creation.
I might have missed this very scene.

I said, "Good shepherd, when you tell me, 'Go',
I am sorry I'm so scared."
"Then remember," he said, "I never send you out.
When you go, I take you there."

When Jesus spoke again to the people, he said, "I am the light of the world. Whoever follows me will never walk in darkness, but will have the light of life." (John 8:12)

LESSON 6

THE MAGI'S EXCITEMENT; KING HEROD'S FEAR

MATTHEW 2:1–21

Note

Before stepping into the city of Jerusalem and the little town of Bethlehem, take a few minutes to investigate the three important figures that revolve around Messiah—the magi, the star, and King Herod.

Magi

Much mystery surrounds these king makers. The Christmas carol refrain repeats, "We three kings of Orient are." Three gifts are brought, so people assume only three people brought them. No one really knows. But a caravan of several magi dressed in fine silk and beautiful attire with numerous attendants and servants, escorted by foreign soldiers is probable. They would have made quite a spectacle riding into Jerusalem. Who were they?

The magi were not kings but sacrificial priests and wise men who interpreted the meaning of human affairs and interpreted dreams.[1] Philo, the historian, recorded that among the Persians the body of magi investigated works of nature to know the truth while also making a study of moral truth, seeing their existence as being a lesson in virtue.[2]

These men were the astronomers and scientists of their day. The word *magician* is derived from the word *magi*. And the term *magi* was later applied by those who claimed to have occult or supernatural knowledge. However, that does not fit the philosophical goals of this particular group. Not only Philo but Cicero, another writer of antiquities, indicated that the magi were truly scientific in temper and genuinely learned. Herodotus, an early Greek historian, stated they were a class or caste of Medes who were renowned for their learning.[3]

Being educated men, the magi could have easily known the predictions of a coming Messiah. "I see him, but not now, I behold him but not near. A star will come out of Jacob, and a scepter will rise out of Israel" (Numbers 24:17). They watched the skies for some astral phenomena that would foreshadow Christ's advent.[4] They found the Messiah's star and their mission, which was to follow it. But why? And what was this mysterious star?

The Star

The Creator obviously set the star in motion. Some think it was simply a conjunction of Jupiter and Saturn. It could have been God's Shekinah glory like the pillar of fire in the night and a cloud by day used to lead the Hebrews out of Egypt (Exodus 13: 20–22). Yet it is also *not* unlike the Almighty to use his *natural creations* such as a celestial object to show the world his fireworks.

God knew the ancients believed events such as a king's birth, a monarch's death, or change in a ruling government could be preceded by variances in the planets or stars. What greater way to announce the arrival of the King of Kings than a spectacular and unusual star rising, moving, and finally standing over him in the place that the prophecy had promised! This would be equivalent to a remarkable event today going viral on the internet. Everyone could see it. But what type of astronomical object did God launch into motion to catch the attention of the magi?

Many theories have tried to explain the star of Bethlehem. One of the most interesting in recent times comes from Colin R. Nicholl and his extensive research in his book *The Christ Comet*. He gives detailed information why a great comet is most qualified to be the star. He identifies the comet as the only celestial entity besides the Moon or meteors capable of covering the heavenly territory over such a short time period.[5]

Nicholl also addresses the star standing over the place Jesus was staying as well.

A long-tailed comet could appear as if pointing to a structure if the structure was located on the visible horizon and the observer was opposite the side of the structure to the comet, Nicholl explains. He states a coma-down and tail-up position is common as the tail always points away from the Sun. Depending on the season and location of the comet with respect to Earth and the Sun, it is possible for the comet's tail to stand up vertically or nearly vertically.[6] For students of the planets, no wonder the magi wanted to see not only where this moving star led but who it would lead them to.

Herod

Though not Jewish, Herod the Great was king of Judea. His father was an Idumean, and his mother was Arabian.[7] He was the first foreigner reigning as king of the Jews, though he continually tried to convince his people he was Jewish. The prophecy God gave Moses was fulfilled in this: "The scepter shall not depart from Judah, nor the ruler's staff from between his feet, until he to who it belongs shall come" (Genesis 49:10).[8] Soon after Jesus, the King of the Jews, appeared under the spotlight of a phenomenal star, the great pretender would soon die.

Nevertheless, Herod was a cunning and cut-throat man—he had been a political survivor for years. He was appointed governor of Galilee by Julius Caesar. After Caesar's death he secured the good graces of Cassius. A Parthian invasion caused him to escape Israel. He left his family in the fortress Masada and went to Rome. There leaders Anthony and Octavian accepted him. *The Senate named him king of Judea.* After Anthony's death Herod was the puppet king for Octavian. Octavian later became Caesar Agustus.[9]

Herod was known as Herod the Great because of the grand scale of his building campaigns. His greatest project was restoring the temple in Jerusalem to even greater splendor than in the time of Solomon.[10] He had hoped that would win him the approval of the Jews. However, by building pagan temples for Caesar, the Jewish people were even more embittered toward him.[11]

Herod was famous for his extensive building and Hellenistic architecture and infamous for his paranoid behavior. Suspecting treachery in his family, he murdered several relatives, including an uncle, a brother, one wife, her mother, two of her sons, and his eldest son. The king who would not eat pork to prove piousness to the Jews was more of a threat to family than to livestock. This prompted the Roman emperor

Augustus to comment that it would be safer to be Herod's pig than his son.[12]

Not surprisingly, when the magi entered Jerusalem in all their pomp and circumstance and started asking citizens, "Where can we find the King of the Jews? We saw his star in the east and have come to worship him," Herod and all Jerusalem were greatly disturbed (Matthew 2:3).

You now have the opportunity to step into the shoes of the citizenry of Jerusalem and into the lives of the magi. When you decide upon your answers to the following questions, let yourself be present there.

Note

The magi had the reputation of being able to make predictions. They supposedly predicted the rise to power of leaders such as Alexander the Great and Emperor Augustus.[13] Therefore, Herod knew the magi were not only wise men, but king makers.

Another reality bothered Herod. The Parthians had chased him out of his country once before. They were Rome's primary competition for power. Then Herod drove the Parthians out of Palestine. These magi were powerful and influential advisors who were traveling to Jerusalem from the Persian-Parthian Empire.

Was a change of government coming and a new

regime by an old enemy? Was that the meaning of the star? Who was this new king and why was he here?

1. How concerned is King Herod? Explain the anxiety you and your neighbors who live in Jerusalem are experiencing as you discuss the questions the magi are asking (Matthew 2:3).

2. What group is Herod gathering together to research the location of Messiah (Matthew 2:4)? How many of them is he summoning to ensure he has a consensus of opinion?

3. How are you feeling as a citizen of Jerusalem, knowing whenever King Herod believes he might be overthrown, he becomes murderous? Are you fearful for your family? Are you worried that Herod could send troops throughout Judea to root out imagined traitors who he might believe are loyal to the new mysterious king?

4. What scripture did the scribes discover (Matthew 2:5–6; Micah 5:2)?

5. This is a four-part question. You are now one of the magi. What are Herod's instructions to you? Why do you think he did not send soldiers to escort you and the other magi in your search (Matthew 2:7–8)? Are you surprised none of the scribes were curious enough to come with you? (What are your insights about all of them while you travel?)

6. As you and your fellow magi make your way to Bethlehem, what do you see rise up on the horizon? Are you cheering, or are you too overjoyed to speak (Matthew 2:9–10)? You have been traveling for many months and are, now, only moments away from your destination.

Note

Almost all nativity scenes place the magi at the manger scene alongside the shepherds. However, this is not accurate. The wise men saw the star signifying the birth of the King of the Jews months earlier. They began their journey. By the time they arrived, the family was living in a house in Bethlehem. The only information we have is the time table the magi gave to Herod. Jesus was probably one to two years old.

Scene

You enter this humble house with gifts from Persia and the Orient—gold, frankincense, and myrrh. (Note that frankincense and myrrh were essential oils used for a variety of applications such as medicine, perfume, and incense burning, and they were worth more on the trade market than gold.)[14] You kneel and place the precious offerings at the feet of the young child named Jesus. You are aware his name means Savior.

7. How are you enjoying the striking contrast between the king you left and the king you just met (Matthew 2:11)? Describe your experience at both places.

8. Why are you traveling a different route to go back home (Matthew 2:12)? Are you camping for the night, or are you trying to put as much distance as possible between you and Herod? (Note that Bethlehem is only six miles from Jerusalem.)

Note

Step through a hole in time and into the future when Jesus will reign as King of the universe for eternity. He calls back to us today to come to him as King.

I, Jesus, have sent my angel to give you this testimony for the churches. I am the Root and the offspring of David, and the bright *Morning Star*."

The Spirit and the bride say, "Come!"

And let the one who hears say, "Come!"

Let the one who is thirsty come; and let the one who wishes take the free gift of the water of life. (Revelation 22:16–17)

9. **Step out of Scripture, and come back to today for this question. (This is a three-part question.)**

Where does it seem that God has been leading you?

Do you think Jesus is asking you to come?

If you could bring Christ any gift from today, what would it be?

A CHRISTMAS GIFT

Dear Lord, I'm giving you a gift,
Christmas Day.
It is something you asked for,
Though why I can't say.

It is torn, and it is ragged.
And its edges are rough.
And I just can't believe
It's enough.

You open the present.
You are smiling, I see.
You are not surprised
In the package is me.

Not a gift for a Savior,
Not fine gold for a King,
But it is all that you asked me
To bring.

Dear Lord, I've given you myself,
Christmas Day.
But what happens tomorrow?
Will I live the old way?

Then I feel your strong arms,
Hear your voice soft and kind,
"Just remember, my child,
Now you're mine."

"I, the Lord, have called you in righteousness; I will take hold of your right hand. I will keep you and make you to be a covenant for the people and a light to the Gentiles, to open eyes that are blind, to free captives from prison and to release from the dungeon those who sit in darkness" (Isaiah 42:6-7).

GOD'S GREAT ESCAPE PLAN

MATTHEW 2:13–23

Note

This is the last lesson but not the final chapter on God's plan for Jesus or for you. As the story unfolds, it seems that the plan of salvation for the world will be destroyed, and then God intervenes. The Christmas story or Advent is just the beginning of a bigger story.

1. List the exact instructions the angel gives Joseph tonight (Matthew 2:13).

2. God's foreknowledge gives Joseph a head start on Herod. Which words of the angel reveal that the search has not yet begun (Matthew 2:13)?

3. Where did they go, and what prophecy was fulfilled (Matthew 2:14; Hosea 11:1)?

Note

The escape of Joseph and his family probably took place the same night the magi left. A large Jewish population lived in Egypt. Joseph, Mary, and the young boy, Jesus, could have felt welcomed there without drawing much attention to themselves.[1]

The distance from Bethlehem, to be safely inside Egypt's borders, was approximately one-hundred miles. To ensure their protection Joseph probably took his family and refugeed deeper into Egypt, until reaching the Nile Valley. They may have stayed in the city of Alexandria which was known as a safe haven for Jews.

4. What horrible massacre did Herod perpetrate in his attempt to secure his throne (Matthew 2:16–18; Jeremiah 31:15)? Who else was trying to destroy Jesus (Revelation 12:4–6)?

5. How did God reassure Joseph of the child's safety and call them back to Israel (Matthew 2:19–21)?

Note

After the slaughter of the children in Bethlehem, Herod became stricken with several diseases and disorders. Seeing his end in sight, he arrested three thousand prominent citizens to be slaughtered on the occasion of his death. He reasoned that no one would grieve his passing, so he would ensure people were sad nevertheless. (Jewish leaders were eventually released and not killed after his demise.)[2]

While Jesus and his family resided in Egypt, Herod the Great finally died. His kingdom was divided between his three sons, Phillip, Antipas, and Archelaus. Archelaus ruled Judea. He was more ruthless than his father. (The people lodged so many complaints against him that Rome eventually exiled him to Gaul.)[3]

Joseph had good reason to want to avoid Judea once he heard it was being ruled by Archelaus. Being warned in a dream, he returned to Galilee. Joseph chose his hometown of Nazareth (Matthew 2:22).

No one knows where the prophecy originated that

Jesus would be called a Nazarene (Matthew 2:23). It was apparently well known but not written in Scripture. Nazareth had a poor reputation and was not held in high regard.

Jesus of Nazareth is how Jesus would be known. He cared about the outcasts and sinners, though he was without sin. Jesus never seemed to mind being from Nazareth. That just meant he was one of the people.

Step through a hole in time, and go thirty years into the future earthly ministry of Jesus Christ, the Son of God. He was born in Bethlehem. He now is living in Nazareth. Where will he go from here? Who will go with him?

6. (Note that Nathanael would become one of the twelve disciples of Jesus.) What is Nathanael's estimation of Jesus of Nazareth *before* and *after* meeting him (John 1:43–49)? What do you think changed his opinion?

7. Now that you have stepped into *The Christmas Story—Step into Scripture, A Bible Study for Advent*, what is your opinion of Jesus and God the Father for sending him to earth for you?

8. **Step out of Scripture, and come back to today for this question. (This is a three-part question.)**

Did *The Christmas Story—Step into Scripture* make these events more real or meaningful to you? How? Give examples.

If you have never asked God's Son, Jesus, to be your Savior, is that something you would like to do now that you have taken a few steps closer to him in Scripture? Please circle one of the following:

- Yes.
- No.
- I am considering doing this.
- I have already done this.

If you already enjoy that relationship, are you ready to step even closer as you study the Bible more deeply and talk with God more often each day? Please circle one of the following:

- Yes.
- No.

- I am considering doing this.
- I'm already doing this.

If you answered yes to either of these last two parts of question 8, write your new commitment in the space provided, and then date it so that you have a record for yourself whenever you want to look at it.

My new commitment

_____

_____

_____

Date:

THE NEXT STEP

First to Bethlehem then to Nazareth,
You made the path clear.
Traveling with you, Lord,
Where do we go from here?

AUTHOR'S NOTE

Writing this study and including you in the scenes from biblical history was a joy and a labor of love. I thank you for choosing *The Christmas Story—Step into Scripture, A Bible Study for Advent.* (Watch for Bible studies from this series coming in the near future.)

God bless you! I hope all your Christmases are more meaningful because you were there.

Books can be ordered at the following addresses:

- www.sedertosunday.com
- www.thebookonbullies.com
- www.barnesandnoble.com
- www.amazon.com
- Your favorite bookseller or bookstore

Step Into Scripture Bible Study Series

This is the message we heard from him and declare to you: God is light; in him there is no darkness at all (I John 1:5).

ACKNOWLEDGMENTS

I want to give a special thanks to Mary Schmidt who was kind enough to send me my poem, "A Lamb's Look at the Shepherd". I wrote it many years ago and she put it on her wall in a frame! I appreciated being able to use it in The Christmas Story.

I would like to thank my publisher, WestBow. This is my fourth book with them, and they have been great. I owe a special thanks to my check-in coordinator, Rachel Platt for the professional and positive attitude that comes through each time she answers her phone. That can't be easy with the hundreds of authors she talks to each week. I also appreciate her help with Seder to Sunday, the first study book in the Step into Scripture Bible Study Series.

NOTES

All scripture citations, unless otherwise specified, are taken from the New International Version Bible (Grand Rapids, MI: Zondervan Publishing House, 1995). NKJV refers to the New King James Version (Nashville: Thomas Nelson Inc., 1982).

Lesson 1

1. History.com Editors, "Christianity," Christianity-Dogmas, Definitions & Beliefs – History (October 13, 2017): https://www.history.com/topics/religion/history-of-christianity
2. Michael Rydelnik and Michael Vanlaningham, eds., Faculty of Moody Bible Institute, *The Moody Bible Commentary* (Chicago: Moody Publishers, 2014), 1,457.

Lesson 2

1. "How Far Did Mary Travel to Visit Elizabeth?" July 10, 2019, http://umc.org/what-we—believe/advent-quiz-how-far-did-mary-travel-to-visit-elizabeth.
2. John F. Walvoord and Roy B. Zuck, eds., Dallas Theological Seminary, *The Bible Knowledge Commentary: An Exposition of the Scriptures* (Wheaton, IL: Victor, 1983) V.2:321.

Lesson 4

1. William Barclay, *The Gospel of Matthew* (Philadelphia: The Westminster Press, 1975) V.1:12.
2. Charles F. Pfeiffer (Old Testament) and Everett F. Harrison (New Testament), eds., *The Wycliff Bible Commentary* (Nashville: The Southwestern Company, 1968), 931.
3. *"A Long, Cold Road to Bethlehem: Nativity: Gospel accounts of Mary and Joseph's journey gloss over the arduous reality of life and travel in ancient Galilee, scholars say,"* L.A. Times: The Religion News Service (December 23. 1995), https://.www.latimes.com/archives/la-xpm-1995-12-23-me-17102-story.html.
4. Lawrence O. Richards, *The Teacher's Commentary* (USA, Canada, England: Victor, 1984), 645.
5. William Barclay, *The Gospel of Matthew* (Philadelphia: The Westminster Press, 1975) V.1:24.

Lesson 5

1. W. Phillip Keller, *A Shepherd Looks at Psalm 23* (Grand Rapids, Michigan: Zondervan, 1970, 70.
2. Michael Rydelinik and Michael Vanlaningham, Faculty of Moody Bible Institute, *The Moody Bible Commentary* (Chicago: Moody Publishers, 2014), 1559.

Lesson 6

1. Charles F. Pfeiffer, Howard F. Vos and John Rea, eds., *The Wycliffe Bible Encyclopedia* (Chicago: Moody Press, 1975), 1068.

2. Philo (translated by C.D, Young), *The Works of Philo* (USA: Hendrickson Publishers, 1993), 6.

3. Charles F, Pfeiffer, Howard F. Vos and John Rea, *The Wycliff Bible Encyclopedia* (Chicago: Moody Press, 1975), 1067.

4. Ibid.

5. Collin R. Nicholl, *The Great Christ Comet* (Wheaton: Crossway, 2015) 134.

6. Collin R. Nicholl, *The Great Christ Comet* (Wheaton: Crossway, 2015) 136.

7. Don Stewart: *"Who Were the Herods?* July 10,2018, http://www.blueletterbible.org/faq/don_stewart/don_stewart_1213.cfm

8. Eusebius (translated by C. F. Cruse) *Eusebius' Ecclesiastical History* (Grand Rapids, MI: Hendrickson Publishers, 1998) 17.

9. *"Herod the Great Biography"* http://www.notablebiographies.com/He-Ho/Herod-the-Great.html, July 10.2019.

10. *"Who was Herod?"* Zondervan Academic (December 19, 2017): https://www.binlegateway.com/blog/2017/12/who-was-herod/

11. F.F. Bruce, *New Testament History* (NY: Double Day, 1971), 22.

12. Don Stewart: *"Who were the Herods?"* http://www.blueletterbible.org/faq/don_stewart/don_stewart_1312.cfm

13. Michael Rydelnik and Michael Vanlaningham, Faculty of Moody Bible Institute, *The Moody Bible Commentary* (Chicago: Moody Publishers, 2014), 1,456.

14. *"A Wise Man's Cure"*: Frankincense and Myrrh—History: http://www.history.com/news/a-wise-mans-cure-frankincense-and-myrrh, July 10, 2019.

Lesson 7

1. Charles F. Pfeiffer (Old Testament) and Everett F. Harrison (New Testament), *The Wycliffe Bible Commentary,* (Nashville: The Southwestern Company, 1968), 933.
2. *"Who was Herod?"* Zondervan Academic (December 19, 2017): https://www.biblegateway.com/blog/2017/12who-was-herod/.
3. F. F. Bruce, *New Testament History* (NY: Doubleday, 1969), 24.

So what do you think about that star?

We also have the words of the prophets
made more cetain, and you will do
well to pay attention to it, as to a light
shining in a dark place, until the day
dawns and the morning star rises in
your hearts (II Peter 1:19).

Printed in the United States
By Bookmasters